PRAISE for *Growing Flames: Fury and Lavender*

"Emmanuel Kane's *Growing Flames: Fury and Lavender*, is a brilliantly conceived poetic feast. The poet demonstrates a remarkable breadth of knowledge and a stirring imagination full of tropes and metaphors that truly make this a great book. Kane masters the history, literature, and moral ethics that makes his poetry live in the present. Using the military and martial examples he brings truth in words to life."

—Molefi Kete Asante, author of *Facing South to Africa*

"With powerful imagery and language, Emmanuel Kane takes his readers to places where they may not want to go. No one wants to experience war, suffering and death, but the world can't turn a blind eye to it either. Many of these poems are uncomfortable and hard to read, but poetry doesn't have to be pretty. Kane pulls the reader from the comfort of a chair into a world of uncertainty, where many people live out their daily lives. This is not an uplifting book, but it is a call to action, a call to care for our fellow man."

—Jonathan K. Rice, Editor/Publisher, *Iodine Poetry Journal*

"Here are the words of no return. Emmanuel Kane writes about war and refugees. Here is the verse of headlines. This collection of poems is troubling. There is blood on many of the pages. It's a reminder that the present is a dangerous place to live. Kane writes about Isis and Miriam Makeba wailing from the grave. He knows the beautiful ones have yet to be born."

—E. Ethelbert Miller, Poet/Educator/Literary Activist

"In *Growing Flames*, he captures the disappointments, fury, and melancholy of a young soldier in a very realistic manner. His poems are multi-layered. Most of his poems contain a satirical twist that provides a deeper insight into war, beyond the literal meaning, and that makes readers pause and say, 'Ah.' These poems will speak to readers today because of the continuing wars and conflicts throughout our world."

—Dr. Sylvia A. Holladay, English Professor, University of South Florida

"Kane's *Growing Flames: Fury and Lavender*, is a collection of 95 poems divided into four sections. Each section addresses different perspectives on war, political corruption, killer disease outbreaks, and depraved indifference. Each poem uniquely touches on personal effects to the human soul. His powerful words challenge us to be aware, to take a stand—to listen and hear, to look and to see. This book reaches your very core with carefully crafted prose."

—Liane Larocque, PhD/Editor/Author

Growing Flames

Fury & Lavender

Emmanuel Kane

P.R.A. Publishing
P.O. Box 211701
Martinez, GA 30917
www.prapublishing.com

978194141610-5: paperback
978194141611-2: electronic book
LCCN: 2016944594

Dedication

Table of Contents

Part I

Growing Flames

Soldier's Diary

Strange Feelings

Which sound will reach you when the world's strongest peacemaker sprays
verbal bullets on the children of Babylon and Abyssinia?

He orders bombs to slash open the bowels of unarmed children fleeing
their country.

Why am I still hiding in these forgotten bushes, strapped with
unused bullets while the Niger lets her banks
to continue spreading Ebola-dismembered bodies in mass graves across the
region?

Islamic Maghreb and Boko Haram keep burning farmers' huts. They
sprinkle bullets across innocent men's and women's and children's
backs fleeing their villages.
Wives and children nervously watch and wail from broken windows.

Sunni terrorists rape ripening broad daylight broad daylight abandoned by
fleeing parents.

Elsewhere, Al Shahab and Somali warlords roast oil fields and coffee farms.
Boko Haram bandits kidnap schoolgirls once freed for ransom. ISIS militants
maim those refusing to bow to Allah.

Will the UN General Assembly stomach the cutting of foreigners'
heads in those terrains?

Will angry words and droning warplanes keep us safe?

Will M.L. King or Kennedy or Mandela or Gandhi raise their voices
against this?

US First Battalion

We were the first brigade to march through daunting Amazonian forests,
searching for herbs to cure your anger.

We saw parrots and pigeons in Vietnam rebuilding their nests.
The USS *New Jersey* and Alpha Boats sailed home nearly empty.

We followed in awe the raw chants of Isaac Rosenberg, Maya Angelou, Rupert
Brooke, Hemingway, Ellison, and Robert Graves,
who spoke of America's other freedom
beckoning the world to our shores,
the stewpot of varying cultures and unmet dreams.

We basked in glory after our veterans revisited Pearl Harbor and Hiroshima.

Then, as I lay face down in dark sunshades
enjoying a romantic massage on Myrtle Beach
a bullet whistled past my throbbing heart
peeling off a tree trunk's coat on the far side.

Now I wish I had enlisted in jail.

The Other Citizen Inside

Clad in my diplomatic coat while climbing up the second floor,
where verbs and bound documents await my signature,
I glimpse imams
studying Lincoln's English from a smuggled book.

I peep through a crack on the wall again to see if they will arrest me for handing out violins and trumpets to school kids.

Some have told me they still don't know why light and dark soldiers from the north travel in separate brigades,
why we hate our neighbors and still want their respect. I saunter to the mosque after their evening prayers.

I tell imams our dead
Are buried together in one graveyard,
and red, white, and blue flags
flutter over their heads,
that their spirits still rise and roam together
and travel all the way back to troubled lands,
seas, and airways,
where they have spilt American blood.

The imams cast meaningless glances at me,
smile, and open their Korans.

Emmanuel Kane

The Vietnam Veteran

Sitting in his wheelchair on a Bourbon Street corner,
an empty dish by his side,
his shabby stripes and stars coat
dazzling touristic eyes,
he watches hummers hum by.

Whenever "America the Beautiful"
buzzes in an elementary school,
his heart throbs like an old dog in search of meat.

Like drunken Santa Claus,
he jingles a rusty bell screaming:
"Show your patriotism!

We accept loose change!" he yells to boys and women
entering the mall.

A terrified,
naked Vietcong orphan
scurrying away
from his monstrous bomb
returns to his mind's eye.

He blinks,
cradling the thought for a moment.
A sweet tear rolls down his right jaw.

America the Beautiful!

Another Martyr Is Born

Abu Bakr al-Baghdadi is dying!
Fresh blood
is oozing from his forehead.

It's been stung by an American missile.

He had just finished watching Al Jazeera.
Wolf Blitzer is breaking the news.

"Abu Bakr al-Baghdadi's bodyguard
is picking up his handset wired by the FBI.
She phones Shaheed, 'We have a new martyr!'"

Genius!
A man in a wrinkled tunic
pushes a captive toward the camera lens
brandishing a knife.

Raising the captive's arm,
he says,
"We will cut off his head today."

Blast!
Fireball!
Another
Al-Qaeda leader
is silenced.

Deadly Recruitment

After having hashish, Marwan and Ismene cry uncontrollably.
They drink tea.

They gulp espresso from twilight
to sunlight while their women with long, dark,
glossy hair cuddle up
with well-endowed coalition soldiers in desert tents.

Arab boys swinging American flags on Arab streets
sing from their lungs as Bavarian, Russian, French, British, Australian, and
Aztec soldiers roll in tankers, crushing lives.

They dance for their children,
for a Tunis trader
who burned down his own body
for peace.

They tell world youth drenched in poverty
while their leaders ship millions to Swiss banks,
"Brothers and sisters, please join us.
Let's turn our strength into a stewpot filled with fishes and nets.
Let's dance and drink tea with Chinese oligarchs.
Let's share our hooks and worms
with the fisherman in Belize, Benin, and Santa Cruz.

Let's go to Mumbai, Peking, and Sao Paolo and punch freedom in the face.

Come now!"

Come,
Let's drink from freedom fountain together.

Sensible Acts of War

Steel guns
arched out from our ships
fly red, white, and blue
to green pastures across oceans.

White suits, muddy boots
sing angry songs, marching toward death.

Ships sailing ashore wave at free Europe.
Tanks roll across the Sahara Desert at night with helmets inside,
fingers on the trigger
as polished machine guns hidden in ISIS creeks
ready
to storm cafés and crowded markets.

Tan faces holding machine guns
sneak underneath thickets,
stealthily looking around.

Black balls drop from the sky.

Rampaged Israeli helicopters shred turf.
Lebanese rockets
land on Galilee's kindergarten centers again.

White phosphorus litters schoolchildren's faces,
racing toward their mothers, crying.

Wild dogs sniff the air and bark nonstop.
Cats and goats and horses
run wildly about the neighborhood,
looking for their own homes.

Emmanuel Kane

US Warship on Patrol

The USS *George Washington*
is cruising through oceans.

Men with binoculars track Somali pirates
and ISIS militants scouring for freedom's blood.

ISIS farmers hoist straw men on the shores,
briefly wading off the shipmen.

Fireballs and body parts disrupt the sleeping sea.

Bhaskara natives rush to the shore calling them Bule.

Busy fishermen arriving offer burial on the farms
without a ritual
as Buddhist monks look on

—strange for these Japanese
who bury their own
with style and pomp.

Scribbled on a Rough Beach Bench

A green light blinks atop a coast guard post
a mile deep into the calming night.

To my left, two rays shining, afloat in the waterbed,
light up the shores, unaware a ship hoisting a US flag
strolling past kissers,
is poised to keep peace here.

As a coast guard boat flies toward a flagless ship,
I wonder
whether the romance from
a poor chocolate boy
adorned by
that Midwest ever-cooling breeze
and oceanic
sprinkles caresses your heart now.

This love-starved Peeping Scribe
working in the dark must
not tarry here any longer-

Those groovy geese
with legs spread all over the lawns
want to call the police.

My Ex-Girlfriend

You birthed boys
while my mother slowly expired in a nursing home
with her back pinned against the earth,
her eyes watching God.

The bloke whom women loosely branded Kennedy
came along and snatched her heart from me.

She eloped to Martha's Vineyard.
Death emerged from a truck and crushed them,
one by one.

But I, sitting behind a flaming candle beside my iron bed
composed countless poems for Ashley and Bryant,
Tammie and Mom.

The next morning
General Schwarzkopf
moved me to Germany,
to the Mexican border,
to Panama,
to Bosnia,
and then Syria.

The world citizen now,
I must plant my coconut tree
in Baghdad.

So
don't expect me home
any time soon.

Ming

War and snow make me feel old
though I'm still young enough to fall in love.

I met a woman at Scholars' Institute in Singapore.
Her name is Ming
Shi Wu, a good thinker.
Because we had pleasant thoughts and plenty of beer to gulp,

we went hiking in the rain forest.
We traded ideas for tomorrow's now,
unearthing and sharing our achy pasts.

We discussed plans for grown freed slaves,
tired Third World men
arriving on Western shores in open boats
unseen
by coast guard speed boats.

We examined the poor pining in Malay's slums
that UNICEF did not notice.

We pictured African economies jammed
in windowless rooms
in Singapore,
some with stinky wounds.

We visited the Amazon
and the blind caves
unsure how Bin Laden
and ancient man survived.

Ming and I agreed to marry.

Together
we will patch their wounds
without complaining.

The Funeral

Emily, do not weep for me.

I am not in that box.
Spring's winds
and perfumed green grass are here with me.

There're no boots, cannons,
or smoke or fear.

No captains or generals.
ISIS, Jews, gentiles, and Arabs I have killed
were not in war clothes.

We wear one cloth.
We eat and play together.

Go home.

Tell Bryant
to wear my decorated cap
when he
turns eighteen.

Mein Deutsch Geist: My German Blood

Boris has said, Ich Bin in Berliner

When Osama mounted the Brandenberger torah,
the world heaved—
Alas.

We will have true democracy now!!

Boris waved the American flag
screaming, "Freeeeeedom!"

Gazing at his swollen veins around his neck
I told him I made Obama President of the Universe
before he was ever born.

-I did not flinch

Boris looked at me.
He smiled wryly and said:

You weren't here when 250,000 Germans
thronged Berlin waving Lincoln's and Bismarck's flags
to hear
the light-skinned Kenyan boy
who had won our hearts wielding words
and rolling his eyes like Malcolm X and MLK Jr on the pulpit.

Some say he has Phyllis Wheatley's genes.

Tongues are still unleashing venom,
'Hawaii never delivered him to us.

He can't be one of us. You'll see and learn.

The Kaiser Returns Home

Wife's Interrogation

Maestro, have you come back to study the books stacked on my mind?

Have you come back here
to tell the people of Wiesbaden
that Afghan villagers have no *brokkoli-Auflauf* and no Köstritzer?
That you have only hashish for dinner?

Have you come
to tell Wiesau folks
you'll rejoin the Islamic Chechnya freedom fighters
if the warlords drop their arms for Trump?

Your contoured face, sand-baked lips, and coarse palms
preach volumes of torture and loneliness even to seven-year-olds. Instead of saying
wie geht es euch or thumbing the pages of my ample body,
you stutter,
you mangle your meal,
you cross your fingers during dinner miming war stories
alone.

You stare at your neighbors walking their dogs.
When Sabine's dog starts to play with her cat, you frown.

At sunrise,
Hitler waved his puppy doll at you, smiling.

You mumbled, asked for your revolver.
You fired at the screen.

Visit to Stefflwirt Wiesau

5:00 a.m.
They stream into this ancient tavern, clad in thick coats and shawls and hats like
Santa Claus descending from the chimney.
They laugh richly, kiss lips and tumblers.
They gulp Köstritzer, Lorch, and Paulaner Original Münchner. They yell, "Yah!
Yah!" to every word uttered, laughing hysterically, sweating.
They chitchat like Zirkov and Co. Ltd. selling arms to Taliban fighters in the
House of Commons.
With eyeballs dilating, cheeks bustling with cheerful blood, they toast tumblers
and sip Köstritzer and laugh and share jokes.

Some order Schlachtschüssel—Bavarian!

Minus three degrees Centigrade outside. Enchanted women flow into Stefflwirt

Wiesau
and join American nurses and a man in a Fouled Anchor laughing madly at a
reserved table.

Sitting around a six-foot-square table with louder women at the far end in a
medal-filled cap is Emil Effenberger,
the never-forgotten World War II maestro who tackled the Russians and won.
The Kaiser strolls up to my table and shakes my hand.
His eyes are fading now, but from behind those sockets,
the hefty stomach and lean limbs,
a stiff fist pounds my table,
a Bismarckian holler, "*Ich bin 96 Jahre alt.
Wo bist du her?*" "I'm American."
"Soldier or private?"
"Professor."

The Kaiser tells me, "*Gute nacht*";
Mounts a cool jacket over his red,
Long-sleeve sweater;
and strides out of Stefflwirt Wiesau into the snowy night.
Sabine in army uniform, whispers,
"His friends and family are all dead!"

The Kaiser's Grandson Putin Beckham, Aus der Region

Boris is a cat.
Boris bought Oskar's cat for 150,000 Euros.
He kissed her lips for 120 days.
She left town and broke up with him—
he hated the text message.

He grabbed a revolver under Hitler's pillow, went on a shooting ram- page in
Munich.

Today
he stealthily walks behind Berlin's high streets alone
dodging cameramen camped in restaurants and jewelry stores.

I still don't know where he left his jacket, the tricky rifle
while on *Bild Zeitung*'s middle pages
I find a festival of ruse words and steamy photos
awaiting the quizzical German eyes
that had also seen the Berlin wall fall apart.

Though some still watch Germany's breakup
on the tired television screens
and bemoan their destruction at the hands of foreign friends
Boris never fought against the Bolsheviks.

He never raised his voice against Arab Spring inventors.
He fights with foreign friends in Syria.

Merkel Addresses Parliament

Have you come back to study the books
stacked up the walls of my mind?

Have you come back to tell Weiden folks that Afghan villagers
have no
Brokkoli-Auflauf
and no Köstritzer to quench war thirst,
that you had only hashish for dinner?

Have you come
to tell Washington's residents
you will join Islamic fighters
if Eritrean warlords drop their arms
and follow Obama's trumped followers?

Your contoured face, sand-baked lips, and coarse palms
unveil volumes of Holocaustic torture
and force us to thumb the pages of the Bill of Rights.

Instead of saying *wie geht es euch*
or reading through the pages of my caramel body,
you gobble breakfast, stuttering.

You peep into your neighbors' backyard
and glimpse visitors arriving with large sacks.

When Frankenstein's dog is playing with her cat,
you frown again,
unwilling to pray for my safety.
Earlier this morning,
Hitler's ghost waved his puppy doll at you, smiling.

Instead of enjoying James Bond or Reagan on CNN,
you grab your short gun and fire at the screen.

I should remind you that German young women will
lure active American servicemen to their silk bedrooms again.

The Kaiser responds:

Let me tell you something-
Boris is the hero.

He is the cat you wanted to kill.
Boris bought Oskar's cat for 150,000 Euros,
kissed her lips for 365 days,
she texted his girlfriend a breakup phrase
before they had dinner.

Though we bemoaned their breakup,
he didn't fight the Bolsheviks alone.

Coalition forces
led by the unfailing Yankees
were there.

She walks New York's high streets,
dodging cameramen in jewelry stores.

I still don't know
where he left his racket, that tricky rifle.

The quizzical German eye
that had seen Berlin the wall fall
now waits for his American belle
to return.

Soldier Speaks to the Kaiser's Son

Couched behind a weak lantern inside this bullet-riddled wall
I, unseen,
compose countless poems for the Kaiser's son.
Boris, Schuler, Bryant, Klaus, Cuddicini,
and Valuev—all are my brothers.

America had moved me from Berlin to Normandy,
from Normandy to the Mexican border,
Afghanistan,
and now Syria,
where soldiers from forty-one nations
are waiting for life to return.

Those Persians
with verbal and written accents like mine
get left behind.

No one gets to hear our voice in the papers.

Now I know
why my sweetheart cried
when
I walked into the ship
and ended up
here
with other marines.

She should have asked my parents
to mourn my death.

Still,
she is
my hero.

Emmanuel Kane

European Bombs in Germany

November 22, 1943.
British bombs
raid the fifty-three-year-old stone-faced Kaiser-Wilhelm-Gedächtniskirche,
shredding her ribs apart.

Arthur Harris
eyes parishioners
escaping through the back door
—ninety-four bombers crash in farms, bars, streets, schools, churches.

Avro Lancaster and de Havilland mosquitoes continue
to raid Berlin,
forever sucking human blood.

2,000 Berliners dead.
175,000 homeless.

December 17.
Sewage litters broken rail tracks,
suffocating sick babies.

But today,
the Kaiser-Wilhelm-Gedächtniskirche
stands tall
in the heart of Berlin,
ever beautiful and unavoidable;
always beckoning tourists to her heavenly bosom.

—I have my own pictures that I took with her.

Antifaschistischer Schutzwall
(Anti-Fascist Protection Rampart)

Berlin is not exactly the same place today after Hitler disappeared.
Old structures blend with new ones—need I name Christophorus Church,
Wernerwerk, Siemens-Tower, Rapstrasse or Siemensstadt?

My eyes can still see behind.
November 9, 1989—Young hands slap a shamed *steine und zement mauer* with
sticks and hammers, killing communism.

Witches sing from treetops
as the Berlin wall cracks under freedom hands.

Border Patrol police with pointed gun heads
watch sandbags,
Nazi might.

They smile at cameras
visiting from Beijing, Korea,
Brazzaville, Caracas, Bombay.

The wall of death painted with blood,
with raw and cultured inscriptions
adorns tall windows with dim curtains
stretched along the streets leads to Berlin.

At sunrise,
stoned-faced women full of family secrets
hit the streets,
some pushing their children in strollers.

They would not shake hands
with strangers or smile at the storekeeper.

The war, colder and cleaner than ice
cuts across Eastern Europe,
teaching the young and the old
how to smile.

Berlin Is Dying

September 1943.
Clouds.
Smoke is sprouting from chimneys.

It's November 22.
British bombs rain
on stone-faced Kaiser-Wil- helm-Gedächtniskirche
scraping her ribs.

Arthur Harris eyes parishioners
escape as ninety-four bombers
crash
in a farm.

Thirsty
Avro Lancaster and de Havilland mosquitoes
raid Berlin,
sucking human blood.

2,000 Berliners perished.
175,000 homes leveled.

Crying faces
race toward the border.

December 17.
Sewage litters broken rail tracks,
suffocating children coming
to play with bruised bullets.

February—16
Siemensstadt
is the newest orphan
on the block.

Dismantling Communism

Young hands
slap a shamed steine und zement mauer
with sticks and hammers
instantly maiming communism.

The dead wall's face littered with blood ink,
inscriptions raw and cultured.

Square windows,
some tall,
some short with white-washed curtains
invade
archaic buildings.

Some of them
here still call it their east.

Das aber ist Deutschland.

Wartime

This granite,
my old friend
is game—it is battle,
the song
of my time.

My spirit
sings *pro patria muri*,
the anthem of my life.

Have you heard it?

Spring in Berlin

Sitting inside this balloon,
I see men jogging through the paved alleys,
women on bicycles disappearing among green wooded parks.

Stone-faced women with
handbags strapped to their shoulders,
their purses handcuffed by their hands
enter and exit stores frowning.

Punk-haired women on bicycles float along redbrick tracks,
their bodies cooking white smoke.

The S-Bannhof, Ostbahnhof, hauphbahof,
tarred roads written all over the city's body
meander away,
some toward
Frankfurt, Munich.

Railway lines,
unscathed,
snake their way
to Nuremberg and Bavarian cities beyond.

Like a flock attending an endless feast in the Amazon
multicolored sharks,
dive into Frankfurt Main
and take off to lands
arid, gray or green.

Not one Baghdad bomb
has landed here.

North Korea's and Iran's hawks
can't afford that.

So America's fighter Jet will not kiss the ground.

Is that the question?

Postwar Monologues in American Communities

To the Politician

I can't stand the sight of Abdullah
ordering a Syrian freedom fighter to die alone.

How many times must they die?
Who throw rocks at rolling tanks?
Who are hurled
into swollen prison cells
like wounded soldiers at a battle- ground?

Don't ask me who is going down next

—I have lost count.
But remember this:
Mohamed is tired of eating cigarettes for dinner,
of gulping tea,
inhaling hashish
in smoke-filled bars.

He will
never ignore prayer time.

Allah
has not given
him his last word

Afterthought

I would have preferred a mermaid
or a pelican unicorn at the helm of your country,
giving me orders to build bridges and link up minds.

The well here remains dry
while a child and woman roam the sands from
5:00 a.m. till 8:00 p.m. in search of water.

Terror dressed in Dashiki and black tuxedos
tells you to find Mohamed in your soup dish.

Terrors ask the world media choir
to tell you it was better than peace.

Like freedom
it allows you to test truth
and reject lies.

Jesus cannot vote.
You must.

So why did you obey Mohamed?

Is Europe free now?
Is your backyard safe?

How much blood must Arabs and Americans
spill
before freedom
can ring atop Mount Everest?

Why did you obey the bush
and Hussein and
Abd al-Majid al-Tikrit?

Tell me now.

Before Dying

I have come here
to spread children's blood
on these crooked, dusty pathways
as they return home from school.

I want to silence all those market women in black burka
haggling with tourists about naked Islam.

I want to blow out a crowded hotel
to gain freedom for my people
before I die.

Shut down Guantanamo Prison now!

Leave my backyard.
Let me drink my faith,
the love of my life,
and die alone.

You,
Evil Empire,
leave now!

Go away!!!

Home

We sit around a borrowed fireplace
warming our hands, waiting for rice porridge
—the dinner we had Monday.

When the doorbell rings,
they cast a hopeful eye at the local sheriff.
We wait.
8:00 a.m.
The doorbell chimes.
Police officers stand holding a folded flag
laced with stars and stripes,
blue and red.

Katrina arrives.
We cry ourselves to sleep again.

The African nation
holds its breath as water rushes inland
humbling towers and farm houses.

Like the harmattan,
it swerves through the Nile basin onto New Orleans streets,
lifting both man and economy
away to the sea goddess
for judgment.

That is her curse on dirty dozen New Orleans and southern redneck racetracks.

The gods have spoken.
Now, Mark Twain must rewrite the grotesque.
New Orleans must tell me
it is still French, Catholic, cozy
ready to love all those colors along its streets and suburbs,
and the blood spilt four hundred and fifty years ago
that built its glass houses.

Remake duke
before Mardi Gras returns.

Baton Rouge

Like a hungry hawk
in a corn-and chick-filled barn,
the wind sweeps across Cajun Country.

Its bowels which once had men and women
dancing around French
Quarters
in drunken stupor and marked bodies
lay bare like a town in the Sahara.

I peruse Bourbon Street
where wily waists
freely swing east and west
like top models
showcasing Gianni Versace in Paris.

There is no godly heart here.

The Lost City

The people that FEMA did not find, the hamlets that sang better blues than
King,
men with blistered buttocks
sitting on a rooftop
ignored by a passing helicopter, dry lips,
vein-mapped faces yelling at wanton-faced police, wet T-shirts, torn pants
stranded in a broad street, tired legs trekking away from home to places un-
known, hungry children screaming for milk,
for Mom.

Moses!
Will you take them to the Promise Land?

They sit around a borrowed fireplace warming our hands, waiting for rice
porridge—
the dinner we had Monday.
When the doorbell rings,
we cast a hopeful eye at the sheriff.

We wait.

8:00 a.m. The doorbell rings.
They've brought teeth and hair samples. Hope they don't match his.

Then, it's Katrina, Rita.

They cry themselves to sleep again.

Moses!
They want to go to the Promise Land now.

Please come.

Salute to All Veterans

You were in Hiroshima, Nagasaki, Korea, Vietnam, Afghanistan, Iraq,
and the Gulf. Millions of you were dispatched there on June 17, 1917
to protect freedom.

You joined arms with comrades from here and across the oceans
to liberate freedom.

Lying in bunkers and rough turf
you wrote sweet letters to your children.
You married, returned to fire.

You swallowed sleepless nights under hot desert soil and breathed icy air.
You plodded through deep, dismal swamps and thick, dark forests, dodging
booby traps
with your eyes fixed on the sneaky enemy.

The USS battleship and Air Force One flutters with red, white, and blue has
taken you to lands far and unfamed.

You have returned home with the flag unstained.

You stand with Lincoln, Wilson, Truman, Roosevelt, Nixon, Washington, Bush,
Clinton, Obama and America.

You are here today, a carpenter, lawyer, farmer, citizen, American.

Soldier,
Colombian Knights
stand behind the flag

They salute you.

Emmanuel Kane

Tomb of Unknown Soldier

Soldier!
Honor to your country is your first love.

Left, right, left, right,
you have marched to Normandy, Hiroshima,
Nagasaki, Vietnam, Iraq, North Korea, Afghanistan.

While waiting in a bunker for the next call up,
you have scribbled sweet letters to your children, wife, friends,
promising them a peace-filled world.

Joining hands with comrades from different countries,
you have spent sleepless nights in swamps and hot desert soil
pulling the trigger to stop evil from running wild on peace-loving people.

With boots unwashed, you have plodded through deep, dismal swamps, rowdy,
dark forests, dodging booby traps and snipers and stray bullets.

You have stood tall with Lincoln, Wilson, Truman, Roosevelt, Nixon, Washing-
ton, Reagan, Bush, Obama.

The USS battleship and Air Force One flutters with red, white, and blue taking
you across waters.
You bring it back home unstained.

Together, we sing liberty and justice for all.

Now that you are home you will say:
"My country is stronger now.
I walk down the street decorated with medals. American fire power.

"I am soldier.
I am army strong."

As we remember you today,
Please listen, my brother.

Dream of the days you laughed together with all those comrades gathered here
today.

Feast of the Dead

This land of no return
is paved with roses and seaweeds.

Everyone there
speaks freedom.

Our fallen troops are there
singing with church choirs.
Some are listening to violins,
drums, pianos,
gospel, old-time music, jug bands,
Cajun, rock-and-roll, rhythm and blues,
Hip-hop, and jazz and nodding.

Others, unseen,
are dancing
with Louis Armstrong,
Randy Travers,
Jay Z,
BB King.
McCarthy
Zhang Muyi.

At dusk they will dine
with Gabriel
while Jesus
continues to roam this place
urging you

to come home.

9/11

The tower came crashing down.
Burnt bodies and
faces with unwanted powder fled—
some stayed immobile as the world
stood speechless.

Two hundred countries an counting,
they still come here to bask in its scintillating beauty.

Do we keep the faith because
we made McDonald's or
because we have the hand that's always willing to help everywhere?

Is it because those *Mayflower* pilgrims planted seeds of freedom
whose fruits we eat and share with the world?

Some will never know.

But I know that freedom has wings.
Like the dove that delivered the best news ever
about the birth of a savior
it will fly and perch on trees
and rooftops in Africa
Syria that only know pain and violence.

Honor Guard

For you, I must pack up a whistling gun,
brush, toothpaste, water, and love and roll away to Afghanistan.

Jostling through rustling waves, swelling waters, swirling sights,
and oceans unscarred by whales and crocodiles,
I will plant seeds of love till
the world is ready
to sing peace songs
with a single voice.

I'll tan and bathe,
sleep and wake up stronger.

I'll waft up the riverbed and camp among the clouds
and work till dawn fighting for their freedoms—
for I am America.

Let all the nations shout again:
"America, you are beautiful!"

Another Note

As light hands over to dusk,
I glean a nest in a farmland, tucked away in the mountains.

Guatemala grandmothers
scavenge for stale food in a dumpster
to feed their grandchildren till they turn ten.

I glean a nest on a tree branch
that waits for parrots to return.

But they stay out all day foraging for food.
They return at dusk and chatter in their nests all night,
none had complained about watching this desert land
devoured by
those Mainland oligarchs.

I am not sure who has made them rich—
But my blood and theirs comes from a place
we never paid for.

Today in Time

Drums beat with the clearest impression.
Ears scramble to trace their rhythm.

Black boys and white girls,
White men and black women
clad in school uniforms, band uniforms
march side by side on paved roads and dirty footpaths
blowing trumpets, dancing, singing,
speaking preaching about a name.

It has been forty-five years since blood
spilt in oceans and mountains and buildings
as it tried to rise up
to heaven
to beg God for mutual peace,
and to cleanse this place fed full with the wrath of a dirty generation.

It tried to rise up,
speaking from the mountaintop, tried to marry race with love,
preached to stones and flowers—

Yet like Martin Luther, Mother Theresa, Mandela, Mahatma Gandhi, Malcolm
the X-man and Christ, it was silenced in the middle of a dream.

Today they celebrate its birthday
across this
Land of the Free
with song and prayer and meditation.

Some are still intoxicated in a symphony of unforgettable memories,
others call out from television screens for Mandela's Day worldwide.

And some wonder why today is a public holiday. Are you one of those?

Salute to Nelson Rolihlahla Mandela on his Ninety Fifth Birthday

The world has inched forward since a six-foot-tall caramel giant with twen-
ty-seven years in a dark hole,
eating clever words, nourishing his soul with St. Peter's verbiage, dreaming of a
place, a day, when all children under the sun
held captive the world's imagination and lit up a torch called peace.

The world halted to salute you as you clung to life, playing the same game for
ninety-five years.

Men in red jackets and black trousers outside the Queen's Court,
spotted on CNN,
march all day long playing their trumpets and drums.

Women and children in natural chocolate, reddish white, fustian pink, tanned,
or brunette uniforms cheer them on.
Can you hear them? Can you see them?

Ibn Mandour and Ibn Athir know how we look.

Why are the brown-whitish ones still slaughtering one another, maiming un-
heard voices in your backyard?

Why are some roaming the streets jobless, mumbling?
Why do they call your people Caucasoid?
Why are some world leaders using Maida, nigger, Israel, Palestine, Somalia,
Syria in one sentence?

Why are mansions and shacks apart in Bantuland?
Where is Winnie?

Why are the boys and girls not pumping their fists or singing freedom songs in
the streets?
Madiba, wake up.

Open your eyes!
See the love you in the ocean's bosom, in the blue sky.

Walking in the Land of the Living Dead

Last night, on my way back to camp,
I heard that Marwan's girlfriend
unknowingly birthed twins.

With her back pinned against the mattress,
one eye watching God,
she told the imams it's not his.

And the fair-skinned women call handsome
eloped with her babies.

He is her neighbor!

He paid ISIS militants
to storm the American embassy

—they refused.

He sent Hamas,
they refused. Boko Haram, too.

He got Hezbollah,
support Front for the People of Al-Sham, Pakistani Taliban, Al Qaeda.

But the Zionists came uninvited.

They dropped homemade bombs
at the daycare center
marched at the Fourth of July parade.

Death shall crush them,
one by one.

Inequality

Standing by a Grave after 9/11

The red, white, and blue flag with stars and stripes flutters all over this busy
place, flanked by cemented mounds, daffodils.

Brown, pink birds perch here daily,
merge with the quiet sound of peace.

Hurricanes roaming the Albemarle
bring iron boxes from the
Atlantic.

Inside Ahmed, Tom, Mickey, Mina, Chuck, and Melba,
standing side-by-side dropped bombs,
chased away fishy boats,
pulled countless triggers,
stopped stubborn terrorists from reaching our fields and malls.

Here they are
still dreaming of Vietnam, Korea, Iraq, Kuwait, Afghanistan,
even Pearl Harbor.

To destroy,
not preserve
their memory
is to hang my words outside
with a category five
hurricane in sight.

When I return home,
I'll tell America:
Don't leave America's name
to trail again.

Make America beautiful on every lip.

Keep America strong!

Make America great again.

Emmanuel Kane

The American Soldier

When destiny's voice murmured to you,
we saw a spiritual curtain unfold.

You didn't know your flesh
had drunk its last water among us.

So you gave up flesh for country.

You in red, white, and blue leave us swirling.
You hear voices we do not hear.

You have lived moments we could not live.

Though your days at the Citadel
cannot escape this destiny anymore,
we will never forget.

The woman
who lost her husband in Baghdad,
children who lost a father,
friends who lost a thrilling soul,
the nation that lost a soldier
will never forget you.

Reposa, per sue merito.
For all your merits, rest in peace.

Navy Seal

You didn't fear death.
Bullets springing from media guns
blast your ship couldn't silence you.

With war-drained brains,
you rode the train around this paradise
never stopping
to see if the gasoline
was black or white.

You said we're the world.
Together
we said we're the world in two hundred tongues
when you marched through Europe and that Middle East
leaving behind democracy
for kings and bees and vipers and mermaids.

Keep on dancing, American soldier! Dance around,

Dance forward-

There are Americans
behind that hill.

Stopping by a Graveyard

Death lives in this quiet place
blessed with fluttering red, white, and blue flags.

As hailstones fall on my coffin flowers
my epaulets stacked against
marbled walls adorn my spirit for a moment.

Before I came,
I did not study the corpses in morgues
—some lie sideways like portraits in a slum.

I can't wait to join other brown, black, and pink faces
from lands far and near inside these cemented mounds who came here.

Before they left their homes,
they knew death is a pathway to freedom.

Baghdad Heroes

Here lie the rough-necked, red-eyed, stolid faces and broken limbs
who stormed Afghan shacks
with heavy firearms
in search of dodging Taliban fighters
crammed in Arizona's military hospital,
waiting for the nurse
to check their vital signs.

Some are lying still in the snowed valley in their uniforms. One
fell on his shotgun.

One was burned by friendly fire.
One went down with a collapsing bridge.
One died with soiled cloth clenched in his teeth. One drowned in the waterfall
alone.

Where are the tender hearts
who moaned loving words into their ears at night?

They are strolling around empty graveyards
with their babies and bouquets.

Some kneel and rise to their feet, aware there are no priests in that wilderness.

And where are their fiancées?
One has just died while writing a love letter

Missing in Action

As I was just telling you
I know where all Second World War veterans have gone.

One drowned from thwarted love.
One gave birth to another man's child.
One joined the evangelical team in search of a name. One lost her house keys,
her kids still in school.
One wired love to a man in Australia and Kuala Lumpur. One bought a net to
catch phallic symbols for her fantasies.

General Schwartz,
invited to a press conference in Washington
to speak on weapons of mass destruction
commended the brigade
for wiping out Al-Qaeda—

he choked on Barbara Walters' microphone.

Hurricane City

The hurricane swept across Louisiana like hungry hawks diving in a chick-filled farm.

New Orleans' bosom—once a harbor for tattooed men and women and naked teenage boys and menopause women dancing around French Quarters in drunken stupors—is the Sahara.

I peeped through the throng again in search of bodies to rescue.
I nosed through Krewe du Vieux, where waists freely swung east and west like models showcasing Versace on a Paris runway.

The streets were peopled with French cuisine.
Irish violins, African drums, and
Sombreros a
pile of broken wood, boulders, pebbles,
lame frogs
learning to crawl.

Roaming the street begging for alms
was a Vietnam war veteran.

He had no legs and no arms.

Remembering New Orleans

Passing helicopters left behind black men
sitting on rooftops with blistered buttocks.

They are still waving blood-stained white cloth.
Vein-mapped faces yell at wanton-faced police,
wet T-shirts, torn pants.

With belongings strapped to their backs,
they trek away to places unknown
like Syrian children fleeing from ISIS.

Tired legs tarry near a scanty store asking for ice.
Mucus-nosed children on the floors of roofless homes
weep for milk and Moses.

Suddenly,
the Mississippi rages in
swallowing up homes and bones.

Storm victims still waiting.

The world watches in horror
as wicked waters sweep away trees and houses.

An abandoned toddler cry staring at us.

His face is littered with mucus.

Even Christians pray aloud.
They raise their coarse palms
toward the heavens shouting:

Send us Orunmila.
Send back our ancestors.

The Gods Are Still Angry

Katrina and Rita,
uninvited
stormed our barns uprooting black and white seeds
like busy northern slave traders in Sub-Saharan villages.

For once
broken bones
with funk and ferment from four hundred years
crawled out from dismal tombs
on September 11
to comfort us.

Families of marines and navy corpsmen
who have been to Mexico,
Vietnam, Normandy,
Tokyo, Kuwait, Baghdad,
and Kabul in masks
wept for America.

We still remember.

The Garden Tree

There is a tree in Baghdad
that grows but never grows.

I see its matron feeding it with water
from the wee morning till noon.

Its dry twin arms
standing tall like ostriches in a reserve keenly
stare at a pair of adults near an ajar door
screaming under each other's nose
as the coffee pot simmers
and vapor rises from a pot on the stove.

Matron arches her back,
hands akimbo
shovel and pail in hand
watching them in wondering pleasure.

I dare not ask her for the pail
only to hear
I don't belong there.

Torrid Diaspora

Africa stops breathing as water rushes inland, leveling towers.
It swerves through streets, rushing both men and goods to the sea goddess for
early judgment day.

Why did Katrina engulf the Gulf Coast,
not Hamburg?

Was this her curse for setting her children
drifting to the southern slave tracks?

Faulkner must rewrite this grotesque story. And Goethe must edit it for me.

New Orleans must tell me
it is still Republican, French, Catholic, or southern.

The gods have spoken.

Waiting for God

With tsunami on duty
we gathered by the fireplace,
warmed our hands
waited for rice porridge
—the dinner we had yesterday,
also the day before.

When sirens rang
we raised our red eyes
to see what the sheriff had brought.

8:00 a.m.

Coast guard workers enter the living room
cradling broken teeth and mushy hair samples.

I hope they don't match your sibling's,
they plead.

A Slim Thought

Standing in queue by this tree of life,
I watch men and women and their children sitting in a crowded room adorned
with tables, chairs, napkins, older couples, and noisy television sets.

Fried eggs, warm muffins, cherries, and hot coffee easily shift from plate to
fork to mouth
as CNN's Wolf Blitzer tells tales of a black boy
smothered by white police officers in a Baltimore street,
unprovoked.

Must I eat with them when the have-nothings share space and time with these
thoughts?

Must I listen to Wolf and his talking heads and pundits?
who criticize the Land of Freedom on television
but return to their glass homes
while another black boy is being
dragged to his timed death
by another police officer?

Or should I join the growing throng in the street,
who for 450 years
only march singing freedom songs and praying?

Must I listen to Wolf or the lawmaker
who is standing behind a microphone
on a street corner screaming for justice?

He once marched with M.L. King Jr.,
picketed in front of his Birmingham jail.

Today,
he voted for the Iraq war.

Should I listen to him or inhale your sweet,
lingering whisper beckoning me to bed?

Narrow Escape

Idling in front of a broken home
Black boys in cheap khakis, jeans, and sweaters
pulled from a sinking boat
stare at passing Lamborghinis
and flashing cameras
with faces locked behind a dismal past.

Their bodies still smell of fishy waters
while their souls
are forever drenched with images of comrades
drowning in deep blue seas.

They await
for Italy's lawmakers
to kill their dreams with a stroke of the pen.

Or give them life in St. Peter's land.

Surely no one knew
they had escaped persecution
from their country.

Scramble for Europe

Boats in the seas with black faces
clinging to ropes,
flanked by coast guard boats,
arrive on a European island
starving for freedom.

A race-coated policy sends them back
as other loaded boats capsize and sharks emerge.

Now, look to the right,
the police are lifting Syrian families off their boats, hastening them to a shelter.

I must get away.

—some know
I'm an arms dealer.

Power and Abuse

Dreams of M

Clean love is like the mahogany wood. It is like the orchid, bright and airy.
It can float like the raft we use to save children from Ebola.

It is the fishing boat arriving on our shores with refugees.

M. and I could be the hard rock wood on the raft. When combat time ends, we
will build our boat.

We will pack goods and good people
and sail back to the shores
where I killed Al-Qaeda students
and turned day-dreamers into believers
of the American dream.

Shape the planks now;
get the building material together—
Chinese wolves and undocumented immigrants
are sucking away their resources.

Emmanuel Kane

The Imperialist

People think all imperialists are white.
But Chinese and Indian ships
invade our mangrove swamps,
seashores, and desert lands.

They hunt crocodiles, comb the forest, a land of natural music with witches
and mermaids, tree frogs, and hummingbirds, wasps, and bees beckoning.

French caterpillars mow away huge trees
to make way for their restaurants and nightclubs.

Trucks hurl away humongous trunks
to the shores bound for Bordeaux paper factories
as Miriam Makeba continues to wail from the grave.

Indian merchants continue to hoist homes
and commercial sites as Kwameh Nkrumah,
Gadhafi, and Mandela fling strong verbs around.

Chinese traders at night dig away railroad tracks and
sell them to corrupt locals
as their own fishermen
drain the river and ocean with hungry nets.

Once again, the Lion, Deer and Fox
log horns in the green forests,
each vowing to save the turf for its own siblings and grandchildren.

I would be afraid to live there
—people say greedy, highly ranked officials like mermaids
could lure me into the deep forest
to pick my own trees.

Those uncanny officials
could turn me into a witch
and ask me
to lead them on a resource-stealing spree.

I cannot bend.

Another Day

Are rich shoppers still crowding New York's jewelry stores
hungry to purchase blood diamonds or something news anchors call L'Oréal?

Are they aware Ebola has already wiped out Freetown,
and turned children into orphans and blood suckers?

Armed hungry juvenile soldiers
fire through empty streets, gathering goods left
behind by humanitarian workers
as arriving Sudanese refugees,
with skinny kids
strapped to their sweaty backs
dump their head loads on terrains
visited by military boots.

They sit on sand with winds
bringing dust into their eyes.

They wait for UN aid workers
to finish counting per diems.

Somebody has not told them
the rebels will be back.

World Peace Day

They brought us dead flags.

And General Peace
who preached about world freedom
and weapons of no destruction
for years
has frozen again behind
the microphone
while speaking on World Peace Day.

But what really happened to Yasser Arafat?
Moammar Khadafy?
El Abidine Ben Ali?
Hosni Mubarak?

Al Jazeera missed the answer.
The BBC was busy shopping for Mugabe's head.

If you really want to know the truth just
ask Christiana Amanpour.

The Guantanamo Detainee Speaks Again

Freedom and fear are at war,
but you'll be in charge of your own destiny.

Life is a textbook.

Read it now before my bombs devour you.
You are the axis of evil.

Either you are with us or against us.

But what's this bush we found
wandering all over the world for some eight years
until another terrorist fired a scud missile
from wanton lands?

Who's the real custodian
of universal values?

Is it you, Al Qaeda,
Mohamed,

Jesus?

Mr. Power

The legs of slavery once
walked through these African villages
picking up men with terse muscles,
women with fertile caves to ride a small ship
leaving behind no tracks
for their chiefs to find them.

Packed like sardines
with only the broad sea watching,
they sailed for months
arriving on shores
colder and harsher than Sahara heat.

Stubborn heads
denying the wrath of bondage
dove into sea
where sharks with open doors
gladly welcomed them in.

Speaking to light skins
who know no vernacular,
eating strange diseases,
stinking like dog poop
they toiled the cotton fields
from sunrise to sunset.

Even the slave hunter never complained.
Why would he?

The Ur Dynasty

I am King Ur-Nammu.
I hear you've been quarreling about my people
spread all over your cotton fields and congested cities.

You tell the world solid merchants broke the core of my mud-brick, burnt
brick,
that Nanna the moon god
was snoring in her ziggurat
when they rolled over the mountains
padded the deep waters,
rounded our caves and huts
and bundled off my people
into the empty ship.

You tell the world I sold them.
Mossi Kingdoms did the same. Senegambia too.
Don't ask me to apologize.

If the hunter returns,
I would kill the slave myself
and save his torso on the deck as proof
those hunters cannot spare the lives of their captives without owners' blessing.

I would catch him myself and send him
back to the jungle whose resources never dry out, the jungle whose self-ap-
pointed parents
dig out the diamonds and burn the farmlands and oil fields and give only their
loved ones limited pieces.

Muscles jump up the rim and shoot eighty points per game.
Caves yield ten babies per family,
some are Beyoncé,
plastic surgeons
and witches.

We can sing all day,
preach with them.

But we're no Moses.

Emmanuel Kane

The New Mayor

Militia men made me mayor after migrant workers
were smuggled out of town in a warbling truck.

And since I,
retired lieutenant Broad Chest,
had once slaughtered children in a drunken rage,
not a single paper could speak about it.

Unclothed druggy refugee dark skinned women
approaching Miami's shore
look on as their children
gradually turn skeletal and expire.

And they wanted a man
with courage and a wanton smile,
a hater of the poor
and drunkards
to restore order
in the windy town of thieves.

So they gave me the town's key,
a pistol and police wear
to patrol the streets at night.

I spotted Jorge Paez kissing a woman in the alley.
Her head and feet were covered with black clothes.

I pulled out my pistol from underneath my rib
and shot him twice in the head,
jumped into the patrol car, and fled.

The next morning
my neighbor dropped a dead deer in my yard-
I can't even pronounce his last name.

I stumped over to his house and fisted him in the groin and scurried back—
but he didn't die.
To hang him in the forest was my dream.
But hunters might find him and an investigation would fine me.

I jumped into my jeep,
winked a cautious warning at my son, Ted
and drove to my office.

The petition to give Shakira and the Browns the food stamps lay at my desk

-I wouldn't sign it just to shame or expose Uncle Sam.

Three terms in office were enough to fire me. Sixty-two years are enough to kill me.

The Mayor's Mistress and Me

My girlfriend birthed twins.

And that Casanova mayor stole her heart and eloped with my babies.

Death crushed them
o ne by one.

Crouched behind a lantern near my bed,
I composed countless poems for Ashley, Bryant,
and fellow murderers.

I received orders to go to Baghdad.
From there to the Mexican border,
then Bosnia.

I love this job!

Letters to Dictators

Open Letter

I speak for these broken legs
and bleeding skulls lying all over this lawn,
for the street dwellers singing war songs all day,
marching with banners
that spell death for stone-faced despots.

I speak for the women, children, men oppressed
just because they carry no guns.

I speak for those seized from their homes after midnight,
beaten to pulp, for pregnant women kicked about in the groin,
left to bleed and die while their toddlers look on.

I speak for babies crying for breast milk, their feeble muscles jerking like head-
less cows
left to die on the floors of the slaughterhouse.

I speak for students snatched from their dorms, whisked away to pain stalls,
unseen.

I speak for professors questioned for hours about things they didn't say, for
scientists yanked from their labs with their stained lab coats
in the hands of the police.

I speak for you out there with broken limbs and no arm—
you whose left leg and right arm were snatched at a rally,

you whose toes secret police chopped at the barracks,
you hiding bloody teeth from a street bystander,
you with handcuffs sitting quietly in the middle of the road, you staring curfew
in the face as beer gets warm in the bar,
you kidnapped from a village bar at midnight.

A light burns above your head.

Arab Spring

Bearded men with broken sculls
were dumped in this deep pit.

Their bodies, scarred and unmarked, emit volumes of poignant odors, while
their loved ones go knocking from door to door,
whispering with neighbors,
and comb the village footpaths asking strangers what they may have seen.

In the town nearby
nameless graves made in the prison yard,
a sparse grass field
that once reared watermelons and cucumbers
pile up.

Infants with naked torsos, and grandmothers
wail outside their tents as idle young men are dumped in
dirty,
squeaking vans in the foggy morning.

You in a UN hat, a furrowed face.
What are you doing here?
What did you do when illiterate soldiers raided this village
and slapped obedient parents and kicked these mucus-nosed children?

What did you do when a Mandarin mind, unclear about the Zambezi.
And its folklore unearthed fishes and whales from its bosom
and poured them in ships and sailed back to Asia, unchallenged?

What did you say when the village boys had their machetes and
arrows burned and got shot by the Presidential Guards?

Why did you stop serving scarred lame widows and girls in these villages?
Where in your report did you mention the unnamed
mass graves spread across the sands?

What did do the Malinke, Peul, and Bororo
living in your sky blue tents
showed you their dried wells?

Take away your truck. And your dictator.

Otherwise Arab Spring will be back.

The Unknown World Citizen

I can't stand the sight of Abdullah
Ordering a Syrian freedom fighter to die again.

How many times must they die who throw rocks at tanks
who are hurled away
to swollen prison cells like wounded soldiers at a battleground?

Don't ask me who is going down next
—I have lost count.

But remember this:
Mohamed is tired of eating cigarettes for dinner
gulping tea inhaling hashish in smoky bars.

He'll never ignore prayer time
for Allah has not yet dished his last word.

I would have preferred a mermaid
pelican or unicorn at the helm
of your country giving orders to build bridges and link minds.

The wells remain dry
while a child and woman roams the sand fields
from a.m. till 8:00 p.m. in search of water.

Terror dressed in Dashiki and black suits told you
to find Mohamed in your soup.

Terror asked the media choirs to tell you
it is better than peace.
Like freedom, it allowed you
to test the truth and reject falsehood

— but John Milton did not vote.

Why did you obey him? Is Europe free?

How much blood must Arabs and Africans
spill for freedom to ring atop the mountain?

Why did you obey him? Tell me!

Emmanuel Kane

E-mail to the Tyrant I

Mr. Strong Man:
Don't be stupid.
Just because you wear armbands
cloaked in military wear
you are not the president.

In 1955 you discovered the oil fields in Amal and Zelten.
You gave forty countries contracts to drill for 600,000km2.

French peasants did not storm the Bastille
because they had bayonets
—they grounded tyranny because
they had one lethal mental bomb.

You had access to Libyan mind fields, not ours.
We stand with Milton, Marseille, and Jesus.

So don't be stupid.
Thirty seven years controlling your country's budget,
walking on red carpets with the moppet,
traveling with countless wired men
doesn't make you their father.

Here you lie wrapped in a blanket
Your pitiful eyes blankly stare back this life
you thought you owned.

Call Nicolas Sarkozy
or Hilary if you have any guts.
Ask the secret French serviceman
to give back your life.

The Face of Terror

Moammar,
forty-two years ago,
you stormed the people's palace, killing man and dog.

Then you crowned yourself king.
Griots sang your praises with a twisted tongue.

Moammar,
you burned huts had chiefs
genuflect to strangers in your waiting room—
you must not like your own blood.

You paid bad boys to splatter innocent body parts in Lockerbie. Why?
Because you had fed their cars with oil drawn from the Cradle of Civilization?

As America and the UK reeled and mourned them for decades,
you sneered and puffed out balls of cigar smoke from a gold plaited armchair,
and called Italian monarchs to ship you their midnight brides.

How could you read Mohamed's law
and still order men
to quench Labradors
in neighboring nations?

Why did you shake Mandela's hand?
Why did you hire black boys to kill your children?

Why did you cry foul while wiping blood off your weeping face
when rats ransacked your home and found evil hiding in every hole?
Is that where those monsters bound for martyrdom wish to be seen?
Do you know the naked face of terror? Surely not.

Please jot this down:
you died in your hometown
with a bloodied face
crying like a frightened Chihuahua when
while Libyan rebels
pummeled your body with rifle butts and boots.

Against your wildest dreams
you were crushed by the Yankee beast
you thought
you had tamed.

Emmanuel Kane

Note to an Activist (written in September 2016)

Today, drums will beat with the clearest precision.
Ears will scramble
to trace their rhythm among their people.

Black boys and white girls,
white men and black women
clad in band uniforms will march side-by-side
on paved roads and dirty footpaths
blowing trumpets,
dancing, and singing, speaking, and preaching about love.

They will celebrate love's birthday across lands free and troubled with song and
prayer and meditation.

Those drenched in symphonies of unforgettable memories will invoke Mandela's
spirit. Television and radio networks worldwide will drone and announce peace.

It is fifteen years since people flew off towers
and met death below, when angry
planes slashed buildings, numbing America.

Their souls raced up to heaven
to beg God
to cleanse our world
fed full with the wrath of dirty generations
bent on pressing down peace .

It has been decades since a young lady from India
knocked tirelessly on wealthy doors
begging for coins to feed the poor.

Like, Malcolm the X-man and Christ,
he was silenced in the middle of his sentence.

Still, some wonder why we have a public holiday for the King.
It has been long since a young man led millions across America, marching for
equality,
forcing gates to open for these Obamas, Marco Rubios, and Tito Santana.

Now I rise up, speaking from the mountaintop,
trying to tie race with love.
I vote to show the world I am.

But they tell me I preach to stones and flowers.

Arab Spring Sings in the Heartland

On a foggy morning, long-bearded men dump bearded, bloodstained bodies in
shallow pits
and take cover behind sandbags.

Their scarred bodies emit volumes of poignant odors
while some go
knocking from door to door
looking for fresh blood
to join Arabs in spring.

They urge neighbors,
comb village footpaths.

In the next town,
I glean nameless graves
spread across a sparse grass field what once
reared corn tassels and coffee trees.

Emmanuel Kane

Jihadist Dance

Tunisians speak of another spring
amid double American military strikes
— two boys strolling around peopled Avenue Bourghiba
tell me high-level meetings
between them
and the European cock will fail again.

They rant about making time for the scapegoat.
They say people speak
without looking over their shoulders
while jihadists are busy luring adolescents to Sousse
to prepare them for Nikah sainthood.

A false saint endears young minds
to dream again,
to live life according to the rhythm of prayer,
to wear with mystical precision their devotion
to jihad,
to donate their bodies to flies—

For their first enemy is white blood—
they must hunt it down and spill it.

Mr. President,
What did you say
when they broke village boys' machetes and hunting arrows?

Jihadist Recruitment

When he is not playing
with the five sacrosanct comedies of daily prayer
or following the imam,
or murmuring his Koran verses,
Tartuffe plods the streets
discreetly
watching Arab belles
in tight jeans and long dark glossy hair.

With his eyes
the jihadist devours the Eve's most attractive jewels.

His radar
catches a pair if plump buttocks
wandering in the shops.

He gives her five thousand Euros.
He begs her to join her brothers in Syria
and fight the holy war against Bachar.

She tells him she wants
to live sublime moments with the great omnipresent one,
to begin communication with Allah, *tout puissant*.

Through the deserts of Gammarth
shepherd and ship gallop away in his tinted Lamborghini.
leaving behind ailing parents.

They arrive at camp
just in time for the evening training session—

on the menu-
How to bomb
the Evil Empire.

Great Return

After touching base with her native spirit,
the young lady possessed by the jihadist soul
grabs her carcass, labors to a police station,
camping among the haystack.

She tells a Catholic nun of her misadventure with Satan
before the commissioner dispatches a team to the forest.

The nun saunters in rosary in hand.
She mutters-

Give them jobs.
Create friendly communities everywhere. Make love with sports and dance.
Do the belly dance.

Allow OTAN
to rebuild the streets and factories and farms.

Give Arab Spring a breast boost.

Give freedom a friendly face like Kentucky Fried.

A Photo flashed around the world

I glimpse a boy sitting on a chair alone,
his feet are hanging down,
his patched face blackened
with smoke from debris.

Unable to cry,
confused and bewildered,
he nervously looks to his left, then right.
Where is his family?

They're lying among broken blocks.
Their eyes stare at the bread they wanted to eat.

He scoops fresh blood from his wet Berber hair,
wipes it on his lap.
He waits.

Once more
I am told a blast cooked by people asking for peace
in his parents' land
has been scattering them around the world
for some years.

With him I will wait.

But who wants Berbers as neighbor?

Palm Sunday

A word stares at a camera lens
unsure whether others might make it a sentence
or just the first phrases of a toddler.

It mimics its mother, unsmiling, unsure of futures.
My word,
the miles Moses traveled
are like dreams of winning a million dollars.

I cannot glean Jesus's triumphant entry
into Jerusalem
as we celebrate his Paschal mystery,
his Passion and Resurrection.

Like you
I want to reach the Promise Land.

I open life's new page everyday
to know how much he still loves me
though I have sinned again.

I thank him for taking the whips and slaps
for letting blood ooze down his cheeks,
for letting them thrust a crown of thorns into his head .

With frail hands
I hold high this branch.

I wave it,
cheering gleefully as his donkey,
flanked by palm fronds,
inches toward me.

I kneel with my hands cupped, implore him to cleanse my space,
my head, forever.

Shalom aleichem!

PART III

LAVENDER

Letters to Melissa from the Battlefield

Oh, Melissa

The grass moves under my feet.
cannot tell me which dew keeps its blades somber
as my unwashed body slowly covers the space underneath this drooping tree.
The grass moves under my feet
The brook down the valley sings and unpleasant song.
I think the enemy is coming.

I want a brook that sings freely and unceasingly
every unedited freedom song
as it sails home.

Here comes a drone above my head.
It's a helicopter circling.

I wave my rifle.
A butterfly lands on my forehead spreading pollen.
The helicopter lands.

Cadets rush toward me,
drag my body inside
and lift me higher and higher
as Syrian military men battle ISIS fighters.

I look down
—fireballs are flying everywhere
some toward ISIS fighters.

Gotta go.
I'll write more later.

P/s

Kisses,
Bill.

On Your Birthday

Precious Lord,
You have always felt your mother's tender love—
You dwell in their hands and soul when they nurse children from young to
old—

You know their hearts when they labor to bring on new life.
Most tender lord, I make this birthday prayer for a friend I barely know but
whose guiding spirit I hug.

Prolong her life who gave birth to beautiful girls, now replicas of her own past,
who showed him the heart of a good mother.

From the day she arrived here, may she know, from day to day, the deepening
glow in the tunnel that comes from you.

Let her heart leap with joy today, tomorrow—
Let her sip wine, open the gifts, and blow out a candle,
each spelling a decade.

Let her blow out many more candles and see her young blow some
For once upon her breast, fearless and peaceful they lay.

Make her deepest fears depart and troubles fade away like a celestial smoke
atop an evening winter castle.

Make her every wish taste like a glass of wine—
And even if you must deny anything, let your wisdom comfort her.

In abysmal moments, cradle her, sing hopeful lullabies as she did those girls.
Take her hand and whisk her away from pain
as she held theirs and walked them to the kindergarten halls.

She may not understand you sometimes.
Tell her in a whisper, "You are a gift to life."

The Shore

You call me crazy
because I'm up at midnight daydreaming.

Perhaps you are right—
no man sits alone on a bench on a dark beach
to watch couples tending their pets,
lovers sipping silence
and taking slow kisses.

At the near end, white boats
anchored along the trimmed shores
infinitely dance to the maddening
Salsa beat

They're not ready
to whisk lovers
to the cozy islands.

Blinking blue, red lights on the US Coast Guard Post
hoisted in the lake's bosom adorn the evening.

I walk along the banks

Below my eyes
These young lovers are using their romantic
tools;
tongue, fingers, legs are all together.

Look.
They're fizzling and giggling.

I have to go now.

These people may be thinking
I want to point my gun my gun
in their face.

The Day After

I have not come
looking for love residue from you.

Since I'm still awake, tell me now.

Are you ready for my endless hugs
laced with procreation tools?

Whenever you pencil me your thoughts
make sure they are pure
like the white cloth
lying at the altar.

When you sing for me,
let loose your vocal cords so that
from the depth of its ocean
it can drift away
from the callous misery
of your past testosterones
and your jittery heart
and merge
with my thirsty soul.

Plea

Melissa,
unclothe
your
heart.

Mine
is naked,
boneless,
Staring
at this blank wall.

Your Letter

The verbs in your letter whispered to me
about my manhood.

My brain is still dancing.

The adjunct for your loose pink robe
is cool as the evening breeze.
It keeps on playing with my senses.

You crept along coarse walls of my soul
halting tomorrow's combat tactics—

We caress each other's souls
in times perfect and rough,
through calm seas and candle light dinners
as Hooters waitresses stand by in the aisles-

Prying into each other's soft souls
we read our souls
as their eyes watch us.

I'm not daydreaming, I swear.

But I can't imagine what
General Schwarzkopf would do
if he found me here alone
while comrades are aiming at Al Qaeda monster
and shooting
and ducking
under American sandbags.

Melissa Listen

My mom moans.
My sisters shriek.
My aunt laments the day I joined the US Army.

They light up my fire
to fight again for our freedom.

I stare at the sandbags
that take
Russian bullets and American war heads
and complain.

I visit the dark holes where they bullets our war heads.

When I'm lonely
I mime American prayers-
those words priests and Catholics repeat every Sunday
about American troops coming home.

I hear new terrorist cells
are cropping up in our towns and villages.

I hear ISIS groups are raiding homes here,
that they rape children, slaughter husbands
and burn temples in broad daylight.

We will fly cruise missiles there
and creep through the deep seas
and delete ISIS from the earth,
and cure fear
and make
our country safe again.

Watch us rock and roll!!!

About the Author

Emmanuel Kane published his first poem at age eleven. He has since published 14 books. His poems appear in *New Horizons, New Directions: Howard University Magazine, Sensations Magazine, Chapel Hill Press, The Washington Review; The Continent newspaper, Profiles International Magazine, Apples and Oranges Magazine, Electric Acorn, Dublin, Ireland; Lynne Reiner Publishers; Symphony of Verse; New Poets of West Africa,* and more.

Kane is a graduate of Howard University with a Ph.D. in Human Communications Studies. He currently resides in Elizabeth City, North Carolina.